THE BLOOD BATH HAS BEGUN,

are we too late to save humanity?

BY, Farzana Prior

This book is dedicated to my younger son who loves biology.

PROLOGUE

Now that you have experienced the first pandemic of the twenty first century, are you ready for the next? Humanity is on target to experience pandemic after pandemic since there are thousands of viruses waiting to spill over into humans.

Deforestation is driving wildlife out of their evolutionary niches and into man made environments where they interact and breed new strains of diseases. Three quarters of new diseases that have infected humans recently originated in animals. It is humanity that is encroaching and destroying the habitat of wild species and not the wild species targeting humanity.

When their ecosystem is destroyed, the wild species migrate to new shelters in our homes, sheds or barns. They become stressed in this new shelter and their viruses begin to multiply. So, it's not the animal's fault for harbouring these viruses, rather the human is the **stressor**. Also, the number and variety of viruses in wild animals is higher in those that exist near human habitation than in those that live deep in their untouched ecosystems.

Endangered and threatened species are more likely to harbour viruses than those at lower risk of human destruction. How poorly we treat the forests, has a direct impact on how poorly the viruses in the forests treat us...and humanity is already paying the price with Covid-19.

The next problem is that we place different species that aren't naturally found together, in nature, in close quarters. The viruses mutate and start to infect other species, like domesticated animals or other wild animals which they get into contact with. These become the intermediary hosts, before the mutated virus makes the next fatal jump to humans.

Long **dormant** viruses and bacteria trapped in ice and permafrost (frozen soil) are making a fatal comeback as global warming becomes a permanent fixture in humanity's present and future. Already in 2016, a twelve-year-old boy died and twenty others were hospitalised after being infected with anthrax.

The anthrax originated in an infected reindeer that died over seventy-five years ago, in Siberia, and its carcass became trapped in the permafrost. In the Summer heatwave of 2016, when the permafrost thawed, the infected carcass became exposed and infected the surrounding soil, water and food supply, and people.

Viruses and bacteria that have caused pandemics in the past, can survive for millions of years in the soil of the permafrost. Scientists have discovered Spanish Flu viral fragments in corpses buried in mass graves in Alaska. Smallpox and bubonic plague are also buried in the ice in Siberia, and this means that when the ice in Siberia defrosts, smallpox and bubonic plague will make a comeback.

Tropical diseases such as Dengue fever, Zika, Chikungunya and West Nile viruses are emerging in Europe. The Asian tiger mosquito that carries all four of these viruses can now survive all winter long in coastal areas and river valleys, and is stealthily moving north and is active in the Rhine and Rhône Valleys.

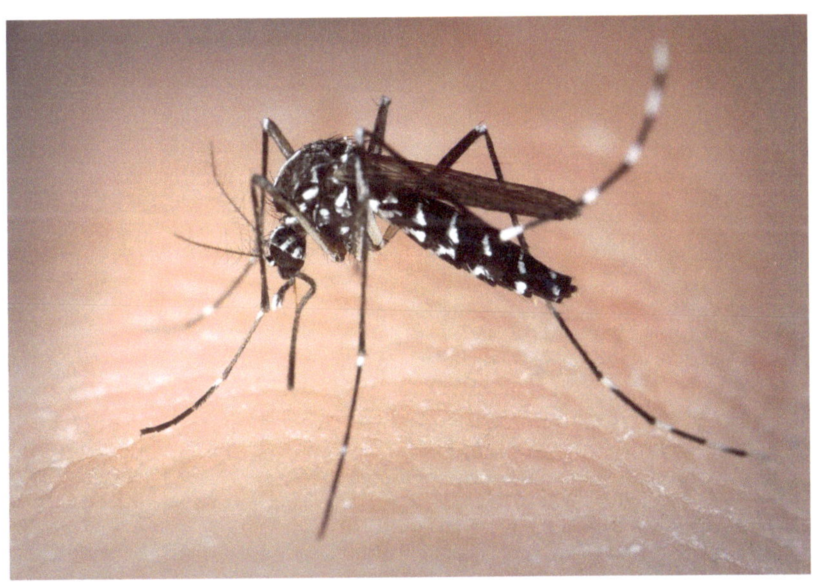

Asian tiger mosquito
Attribution: James Gathany/CDC / Public domain

Further north, in the Baltic, the deadly Vibrio bacteria blooms whenever water surface temperatures rise above fifteen degrees Celsius. Average temperatures are on the rise in higher altitudes and latitudes, meaning ticks can live in new places bringing with them Lyme disease and tick-borne encephalitis (inflammation of the brain).

Ixodes ricinus, spreads Lyme disease and encephalitis
Attribution: James Lindsey at Ecology of Commanster / CC BY-SA
(https://creativecommons.org/licenses/by-sa/2.5)

Are we too late? Nature is already backfiring! Let's call humanity together to make changes toward a common planetary goal…

POLITICIANS: A CALL TO ACTION

Countries are still dependent on coal to provide electricity. Not only are carbon emissions contributing to global warming, but it is also a big contributor to respiratory illnesses, death, crop failure and malnutrition. When coal is burned for electricity, carbon dioxide is released. Carbon dioxide remains in Earth's atmosphere and absorbs solar radiation, effectively cooking the earth.

Rising temperatures leads to climate change which results in droughts, floods, deadlier hurricanes, heat waves, water shortages, pests and fires. In Australia, the bushfires of 2019-2020 caused a change in weather patterns resulting in dry lightning storms and fire tornadoes.

Humid heat waves are becoming more common despite predictions that this effect is decades away. Humid heat waves are formed when rising temperatures cause increased water evaporation from the ocean. Coastal areas are initially affected, and wind can spread the humid air into the interior.

Humid heat waves are deadly because our bodies use the sweating process to cool down. In the presence of humidity, sweating becomes less efficient. Naturally, these populations would then seek out shade or air conditioning, but what if there is no access to shade or air conditioning? Populations will then be forced to migrate to cooler areas, giving rise to conflict as they move across borders.

High levels of air pollution, caused by burning coal for electricity, is associated with exacerbations of asthma, lung cancer, and heart attacks, including skin allergies. Skin allergies increase when clothing is hung outside to dry and pollutants in the air adhere to these garments, which then irritate the skin when worn. Heart attacks increase because air pollution causes blood to clot. Lung cancers increase because air pollution changes lung tissue DNA.

Deaths are also due to the spread of mosquito borne diseases such as malaria and dengue fever and yellow fever. Vaccines for dengue fever and yellow fever do exist, while the malaria vaccine is being piloted, and aimed at children, because malaria is still the biggest killer of children worldwide.

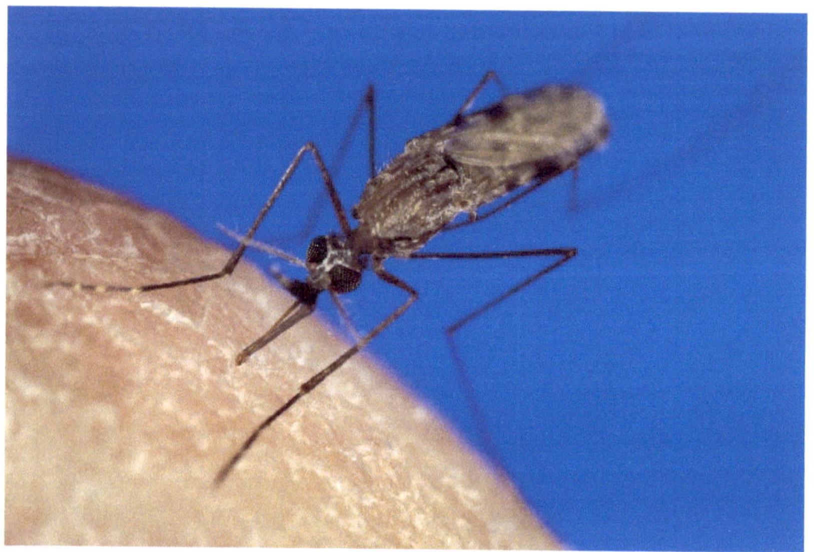

Anopheles gambiae mosquito spreads Malaria
Attribution: James D. Gathany / Public domain

Deaths are also caused by crop failure. Throughout history, when crops fail, people have been forced to migrate and this triggers conflict. Hot ambient temperatures also cause pests to breed more frequently, which in-turn damage crop and spread diseases.

High carbon dioxide levels reduce the levels of zinc, iron and protein in crops such as wheat, rice, corn and soybean. If populations don't have access to meat as a food source, these low nutrition crops will exacerbate malnutrition.

If countries continue to burn coal for electricity, they will need to allocate more funding for disease management and disaster management. However, they will not need to if they are proactive.

Governments and politicians that are proactive about renewable energy show consideration for the health of the citizens, as well as consideration for our planet. Renewable energy may be perceived as expensive, but it is not as expensive as the funding required for disease management and disaster management.

Countries that care for their citizens are, for example, **Iceland** where almost all of the energy in Iceland comes from renewable sources such as geothermal and hydroelectric power generation. Granted, not every country has hot springs and volcanoes, but this does point to the sheer political will of the politicians of Iceland to dig wells a mile deep into the crust of the earth (where rock is in hot liquid form) to access the steam to drive turbines, to generate renewable electricity.

Sweden makes use of hydropower and bioenergy for electricity and heating. This country has abundant moving water and has utilised this to construct a number of hydroelectric power stations. Bioenergy is created when garbage is burned to create heat, which creates steam to turn the power-generating turbines. Over fifty percent of Sweden's trash is disposed of in this way. A further forty nine percent of trash is recycled, and only one percent of trash lands up in landfills.

While burning trash does release carbon dioxide into the air, it releases half of the carbon dioxide that burning coal releases. And burning coal doesn't have the benefit of disposing of trash.

The **United Kingdom** is well placed to make use of wind power generation. In February 2020, the UK has generated approximately eight thousand megawatts in offshore wind capacity and in 2025 expects to add an additional ten thousand megawatts via the construction of more wind farms.

Uruguay has invested heavily in both wind and solar energy, without using subsidies or increasing costs to the consumer.

Through sheer political will, this country put regulations into place that made use of private-public partnerships to drive energy production from renewable energy and, within ten years, now have ninety five percent of their energy being produced from renewable energy sources. The other five percent comes from hydropower which depends on seasonal rains. Thermal power is used only for peak demands and is fired by oil and gas, which is still more efficient than coal.

Politicians, act now: stop burning coal for energy and start burning trash. Burning trash has many benefits and few drawbacks. The most significant drawback is the production of ash as a by-product, most of which can be recycled for use in road construction. Any toxic fly ash can be deposited into landfills designed to handle such materials. Air emissions from trash power plants, can be cleaned through filtration and scrubbing mechanisms.

Politicians, act now: make use of wind and solar renewable energy sources. Don't convince yourself that renewable energy is too expensive. Burning coal is no longer an option because humanity and the oceans are literally being cooked and poisoned to death from carbon dioxide.

Politicians, act now: we don't have space for landfills. We need them for farming, for housing eight billion people, and for growing new forests. Forests will absorb carbon dioxide and will make humanity resilient to droughts, floods and hurricanes.

Politicians, act now: enforce mandatory vaccinations. Vaccinations will make humanity resilient to diseases, and preventing diseases is far cheaper than treating them.

Politicians, act now: discourage war and conflict in your country. Provide for the people by encouraging ethical businesses to take hold, build forests, introduce renewable energy sources, build renewable housing, build infrastructure and incentivise farmers to farm food for the nation.

Politicians, your purpose is to act with courage and ethics as you make planetary changes to your country's infrastructure. You know that renewable energy is untapped in your country, but you fear protests from coal mine workers, for example. Proceed with courage, ethics, and transparency!

ECONOMIES: A CALL TO CHANGE

Global warming is taking its toll on farming. The Spring season is getting warmer and wetter, and the Summer season is getting hotter and drier. Corn farmers are finding that traditional planting windows are no longer workable. Farming is becoming more unpredictable and fluctuating weather patterns means there is not enough food being produced to feed everyone.

Trees are chopped down and forests are destroyed in the search for arable land. Brazil, for example, is the largest beef exporter in the world, and the animal feed used is 80% soy. The forest is being cleared to grow the soy required to feed the cattle.

Deforestation in the Maranhão state, Brazil, in 2016
Attribution: Ibama from Brasil / CC BY
(https://creativecommons.org/licenses/by/2.0)

Deforestation in the **Brazilian Amazon** has now surged to the highest rate in the last decade, with the number of forest fires in the Amazon having increased in 2019, sending dense smoke all the way to São Paulo. The Amazon rainforest does not burn naturally, which means that these forest fires are due directly to human activity.

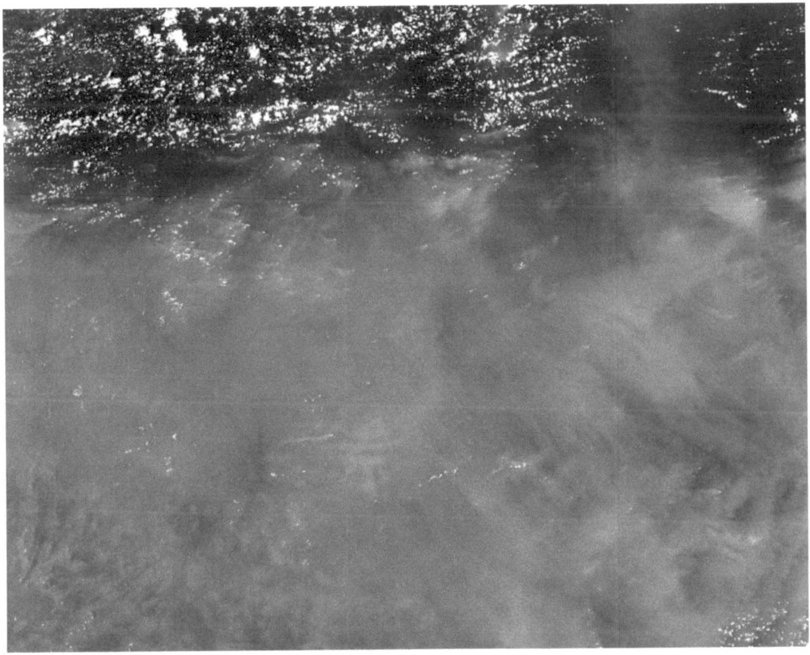

This image shows the consequence of forest clearing in the Amazon: thick smoke that hangs over the forest.
Attribution: Jesse Allen and Robert Simmon / Public domain

The fragile Amazon needs to be protected because of its beauty and biodiversity. It also creates half of its own rainfall, which is supplied to neighbouring farms and cities. In fact, the Amazon absorbs two billion tons of carbon dioxide a year (twenty five percent of the earth's carbon dioxide emissions), which makes it vital to protect. Theoretically, if we could create three more Amazon rain forests, one hundred percent of the planet's current carbon dioxide emissions would be absorbed.

The Amazon operates just like a pair of **lungs**. It takes in carbon dioxide and releases oxygen. Without lungs, humans will not survive, and neither will mankind survive without the Amazon.

The Amazon's hydrological engine also plays a role in regional, as well as global, climate. Water released by the plentiful plants and trees into the atmosphere creates its own clouds and rainfall, which fills the nutrient-rich Amazon rivers and which, in turn, flows into the Atlantic Ocean. The rivers pick up nutrients along the way, such as soil, minerals, plant material, dead animals and this flows into the ocean, feeding the plankton and in turn the fish.

Aerial view of the Amazon Rainforest, near Manaus, the capital of the Brazilian state of Amazonas.
Attribution: Neil Palmer/CIAT / CC BY-SA
(https://creativecommons.org/licenses/by-sa/2.0)

In addition to these benefits, it is surprising to learn that hundreds of prescription molecules have come from the plants and animals in the Amazon rainforest. These include cancer fighting drugs that are so important they are classified as essential medicine by the World Health Organisation.

Some countries have started reforesting projects, for example, **Australia**. The wet tropics of Northern Queensland is being reforested with indigenous trees, with the intention of connecting habitats and creating corridors for the endangered Southern Cassowary and Mahogany Glider. Australia is making use of the Miyawaki method of building forests.

The **Miyawaki method** stemmed from reforestation mistakes made by the Japanese after their World War 2 tree planting efforts focused on using only one or two tree species that were all the same height, and evenly spaced apart. The landscape looks natural but displays very little biodiversity. Walking in the woods, there is an eerie silence. There is no undergrowth, and the soil is dry and hard. This type of reforestation is sterile and doesn't attract wildlife. Too many evergreen trees mean no leaf litter, and organic material doesn't reach the forest floor and doesn't reach the rivers. Hence, no fish can be sustained in these rivers.

Reforestation is not just about planting trees. The Miyawaki method of planting forests builds ecosystems. These forests are diverse, with the use of hundreds of indigenous plant species. This would mean planting trees of different heights together with an indigenous brush on the ground. Designing and planting for diversity, opens the door for other species to follow.

Afforestation at Kanakakunnu, Miyawaki forest - 9 months after planting
Attribution: BemanHerish / CC BY-SA
(https://creativecommons.org/licenses/by-sa/4.0)

Wind pollination and pollination through birds, brings in more biodiversity, and diversity creates resilience to climate change. The Miyawaki method also makes use of soil fertilisation through natural materials of decomposed wood chips, decomposed plant matter and humus, before planting young shoots. After three years, the forest no longer needs human intervention and will grow independently for centuries. Take a look at this link to learn more about the Miyawaki method of growing forests:

https://www.lovely-cards.com/blog/post/mitigating-carbon-foot-print-the-miyawaki-way/

Plants and trees are also important to help reverse climate change, because they remove carbon dioxide from the air through a process called photosynthesis. After photosynthesis, the carbon goes through a process called **soil carbon sequestration**, which is a process where water, or rain, dissolves organic carbon and takes it deep into the soil, as much as six feet deep, where it is physically and chemically bound to minerals. A quarter of the carbon on Earth is stored underground, which means that we can make use of this method to remove carbon from the atmosphere.

Soil carbon sequestration can be made use of immediately, to remove carbon dioxide from the air, and has the additional benefits of improving soil health and improving crop yield without stressing land or water resources. But while soil can store large amounts of carbon, moist ecosystems store more carbon than dry ecosystems.

In desert climates or dry forests, where rain is scarce and where there is a high level of evaporation, reactive minerals bind to only six percent of the soil's organic carbon. **Wet forests**, on the other hand, can have as much as fifty percent of their carbon bound by reactive chemicals. With thick layers of organic matter, water will leach carbon and transport it underground.

Trees are important for carbon sequestration because they can store carbon for many years. Soil is more important because it can store carbon for thousands of years. Plants and trees contain large roots, and these also store carbon. The rotting leaves and organisms living in the soil also contain carbon. Wet forests sequester twice as much carbon underground than above ground. Forests therefore provide carbon 'sinks' by removing carbon dioxide from the air and storing them underground.

Dr Miyawaki also observed that during the **Fukushima earthquake** of 2011, the structures that were alongside forests, were spared the damage of the waves. Dr Miyawaki has copied this and has planted tree-walls against tsunamis and cyclones to limit soil erosion. As a botanist, Dr Miyawaki, is single-handedly helping our planet become resilient.

Farming also needs to become resilient, since agriculture and fisheries are highly dependent on the climate. Increases in temperature and carbon dioxide can increase the yield of crops in some places, but for these benefits to be achieved the nutrient levels, soil moisture, availability of water needs to be addressed. Frequency of droughts and floods are posing challenges to farmers. Heat waves directly affect livestock and causes reduced fertility, reduced milk supply, susceptibility to disease and even death.

Therefore, traditional farming needs to become "Smart farming". **Smart farming** uses modern technology, such as IoT (Internet of Things), which turns agriculture into precision agriculture. IoT makes use of sensors and devices installed on the farm that are linked to GPS.

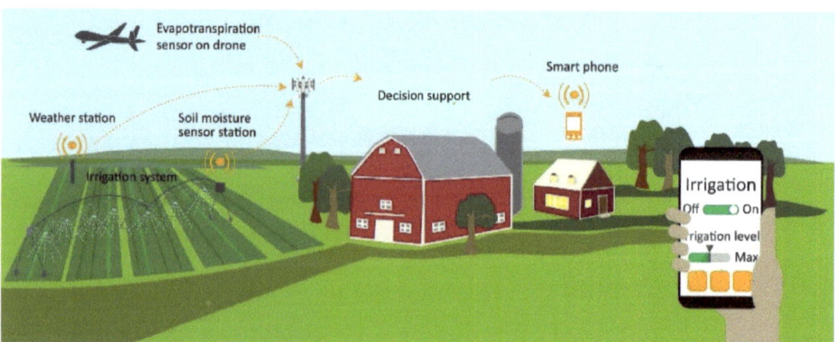

Source: GAO. | GAO-20-128SP

Weather, soil moisture, and evapotranspiration data are collected and sent remotely to a decision support system, which then provides actionable information to the farmer.
Attribution: U.S. Government Accountability Office from Washington, DC, United States / Public domain

These sensors detect light, humidity, temperature, soil moisture, soil content, crop growth and rainfall, and can irrigate, fertilise and apply pesticide accordingly, as can be seen in the picture below.

These applications bring down the cost of production because it can analyse crop yield, soil erosion and diagnosis of diseases.

Plant protection drone
Attribution: DJI-Agras, Pixabay

IoT can also be used to monitor cattle health by placing sensors inside the stomach of the cow, looking at eating habits, grazing patterns and movements, transmitted via WiFi. The farmer will receive a text message when the cow has a fever, for example, so action can be taken quickly to treat or isolate the cow. Smart farming is essential to help farmers address the variability induced through climate change, which would otherwise reduce the crop yield or compromise the health of livestock.

In **Australia**, the government has allocated sixty million dollars to encourage Smart farming. In **Ireland**, Smart farming led to a twenty one percent saving in pasture management, and increased soil fertility represented a forty seven percent saving. **France** aims to strengthen research looking at agriculture and climate, with a view to develop precision agriculture and to create innovation incubators.

Farming is not only about being smart and precise. Farmers also need to phase out crops that are water intensive. The five most **water intensive crops** are rice, soy, cotton, sugarcane and wheat. These crops need to ultimately be banned. Rice consumes five thousand litres of water per kilogram of grain produced. This water could have been better used for drinking, hygiene and for watering drought tolerant crops. Examples of drought tolerant crops are Lima beans, black-eyed peas, quinoa, mustard greens, okra, summer squashes, sunflowers, heatwave II tomatoes and sweet potato.

Most sorghum varieties are heat and drought tolerant. Certain varieties are used for grain production for human consumption, other varieties may be used as forage for livestock, and some varieties are dual purpose. Sorghum can replace corn and soy.

When talking of farming, we also need to consider the farming of fish. The warming of the oceans, as well as overfishing, are disrupting the ecosystems of fish and shellfish. We should no longer be fishing from the ocean. In fact, with reduced fish numbers, we need to restock it. Our source of fish can instead come from aquaculture, which is the farming of fish and shellfish raised offshore, or onshore, or on land, for restocking the wild or for consumption.

While **China's** history of aquaculture is 2000 years old, in the last century it has become the largest area of farmed growth, with farmed seafood accounting for over half of China's seafood production. Farmed seafood sources are a far better alternative than fishing from the ocean.

The Atlantic salmon is the top farmed fish in **Norway**, representing over eighty percent of the country's aquaculture production, and

Vietnam is one of the top producers of farm-raised crustaceans. Aquaculture can become the norm, and fishing from the ocean can then become a rare occurrence.

Salmon farm in the archipelago of Finland
Attribution: Plenz / CC BY-SA (https://creativecommons.org/licenses/by-sa/3.0) / CC BY-SA (https://creativecommons.org/licenses/by-sa/3.0)

Countries that are on the **shame list** for over-fishing tuna in the pacific are Japan, China, the US, Indonesia, Chinese Taipei and South Korea. Fishermen are of the belief that killing an animal that is on top of the food chain (for example, sharks, tuna and whales) will increase the yield of fish in the ocean. Little do they know that the faeces of whales are a food source for plankton, and plankton is the food source that supports all marine life. Little do they also know that sharks keep the oceans clean by consuming weak and sick marine life, and by keeping the marine food chain in check.

Economists, this is a call to incentivise Smart farming methods, so that crop and livestock can be kept disease free, while increasing crop yield, and with minimal use of pesticide, water and fertiliser.

Economists, this is a call to ban the burning and destruction of forests, and to incentivise innovative solutions for meeting the nutritious food requirements of both humanity and their livestock.

Economists, this is a call to incentivise the planting of Miyawaki forests, in close proximity to farms and cities, to protect the cities and farms from climatic disasters and to produce oxygen for the people.

Economists, this is a call to incentivise the planting of crops that are disease resistant, drought resistant and flood resistant, and yet are delicious and nutritious, and safe for both livestock and human consumption, and to ban crop that requires too much water.

Economists, this is a call to ban pesticides that are toxic to the environment, and to fine farmers that use damaging pesticides.

Economists, your purpose is to operate with integrity and ethics! Build forests to increase economic resilience to floods and droughts and introduce renewable farming methods, even if these changes are deemed to be too expensive!

SOCIETY: A CALL TO CARE

Another way to become resilient to climate change is through vaccinations. Global warming is contributing to the spread of pathogens (diseases). Ticks and mosquitos are increasing in numbers and are colonising new areas. As temperatures rise and conditions change, virulent pathogens are emerging.

Let's take a step back to describe how our bodies respond to a pathogen. When pathogens enter the body, the body's immunity responds by producing antibodies. These antibodies fight the pathogen and protects against further infection. A healthy person can fight pathogens so efficiently that he may never become aware that he was even exposed to a pathogen.

When a person's immunity faces a brand-new pathogen, it takes a few days to produce antibodies. For really nasty viruses and bacteria, like measles and whooping cough, a few days is too long, and the pathogen can kill the person before antibodies are produced.

That is where **vaccines** come in. Vaccines prepare the body to fight disease without exposing the body to the disease. The foreign particle in the vaccine looks like the pathogen but isn't the pathogen, so it's a lookalike, and the immunity produces antibodies to the lookalike.

These antibodies are stored in the memory of the body's immunity for use on another day. When the body is then exposed to the real pathogen it produces an immune response from memory, and can quickly produce the same antibodies for the real pathogen as it had safely done for the lookalike. This antibody response is so quick that the person is saved from death.

Vaccines also work on a community level. When more than ninety percent of the community has immunity, the unvaccinated people don't get sick because there is strength in numbers, and it is highly unlikely that unvaccinated people will get exposed to another person with that disease. When most of the community is vaccinated this is called **herd immunity**. Herd immunity is vital, as it helps to protect those that cannot be vaccinated because they are too young or if their immunities are too weak.

Anti-vaxxers benefit from herd immunity. They don't vaccinate and they don't get sick. They then erroneously believe that vaccines have no benefit because they haven't been vaccinated and they didn't get sick. When more in the community don't vaccinate, herd immunity is lost. This means that those that are vaccinated will survive and those that are not vaccinated will succumb.

Pictures convey a thousand words and the following pictures of vaccine preventable diseases will remind us, as well as anti-vaxxers, of the dangers of not vaccinating. The following diseases are already making a comeback.

- **Polio** is a potentially deadly virus, and if a person doesn't die from the poliovirus, then he will be permanently paralysed as the poliovirus invades the body's brain and spinal cord.

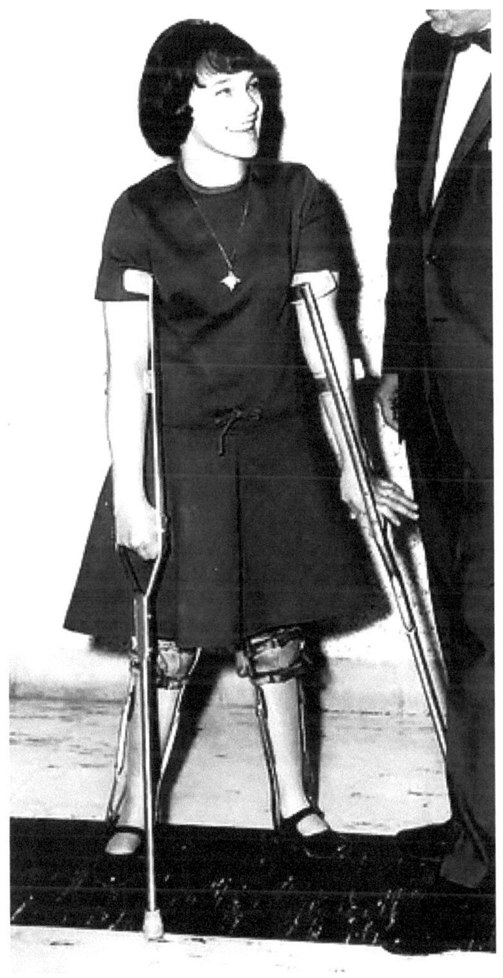

- **Tetanus** causes painful muscle stiffness and lockjaw, and this can be fatal. A person can be exposed when a contaminated piece of metal grazes or cuts the skin.

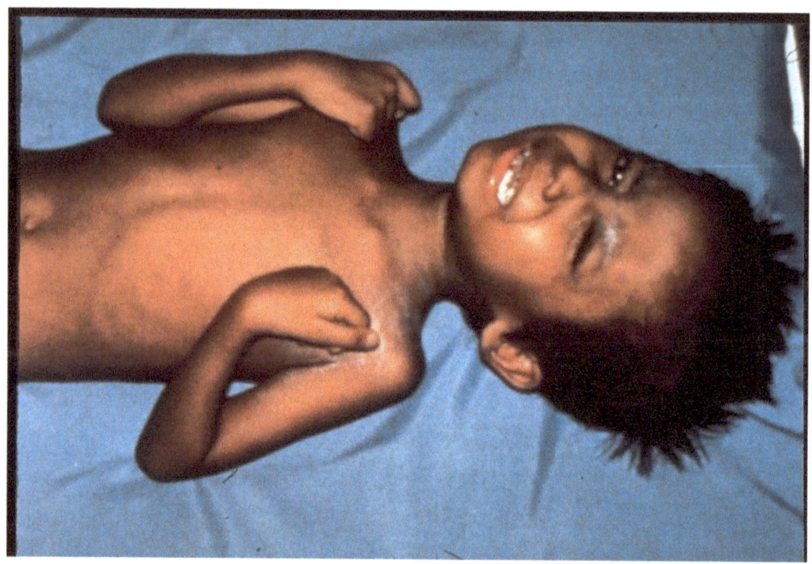

Child has painful muscle contractions from tetanus (Source: World Health Organization)

- **Hepatitis B** is spread through blood or bodily fluids, and inflames the liver. It is especially dangerous to babies who become infected from the mother during childbirth.

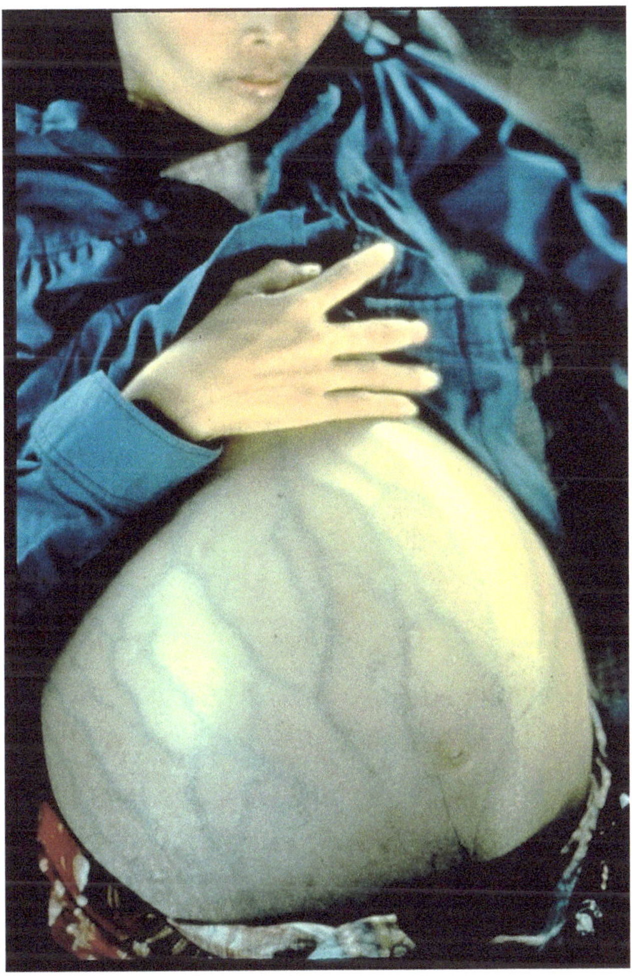

This woman is suffering from liver cancer caused by hepatitis B (Source: Centers for Disease Control and Prevention)

- **Hepatitis A** is a contagious liver disease, and is transmitted through person to person contact, or through contaminated food or water.

Man with jaundice (yellowing of skin and eyes) (Source: Centers for Disease Control and Prevention)

- **German measles** (rubella) is spread by coughing and sneezing. It is especially dangerous to a pregnant woman and her unborn baby. If unvaccinated pregnant women are exposed to German measles, the baby can die or can develop serious birth defects.

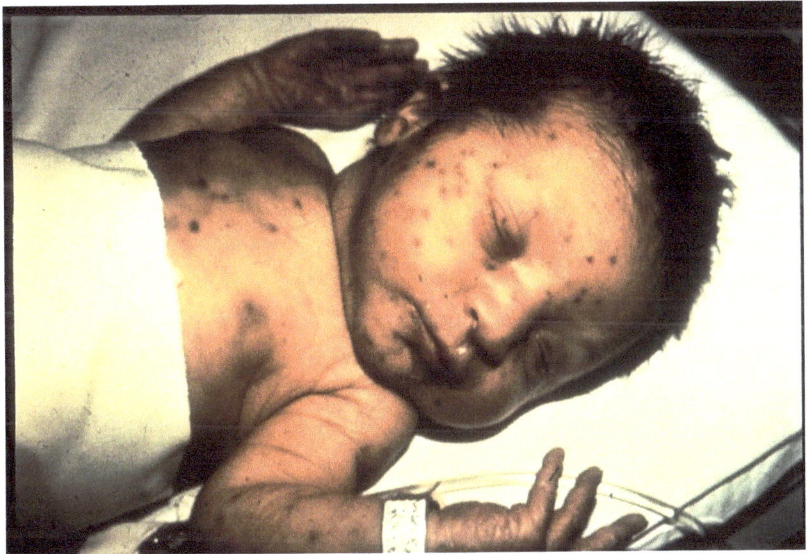

Infant with congenital rubella syndrome (Source: Centers for Disease Control and Prevention)

- Haemophilus Influenzae type B (**Hib meningitis**) can do serious damage to a child's immune system and can cause brain damage, hearing loss and death.

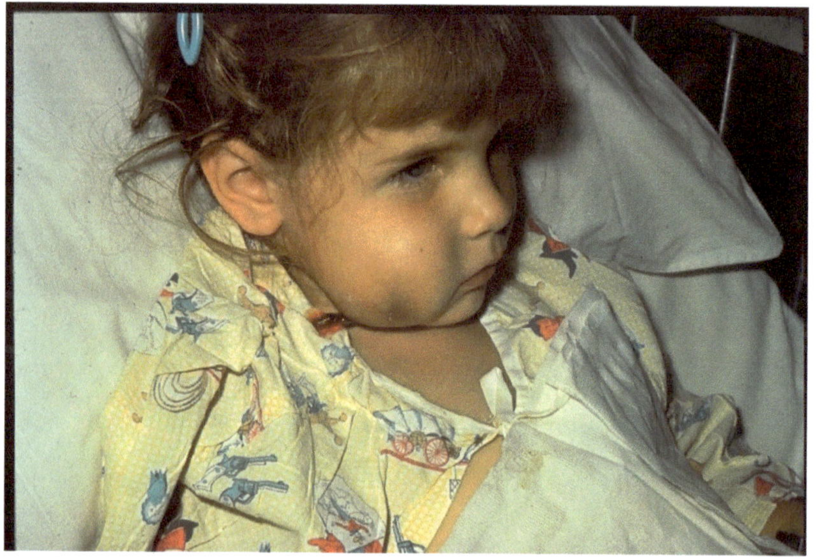

Child has swollen face due to Hib infection (Source: Children's Immunization Project, St. Paul, Minnesota)

- **Measles** is so contagious that people walking into a room 2 hours after the measles-infected person has left the room, will become infected. Measles is a respiratory condition that presents with total body skin rash and flu like symptoms. Pneumonia is a complication of measles.

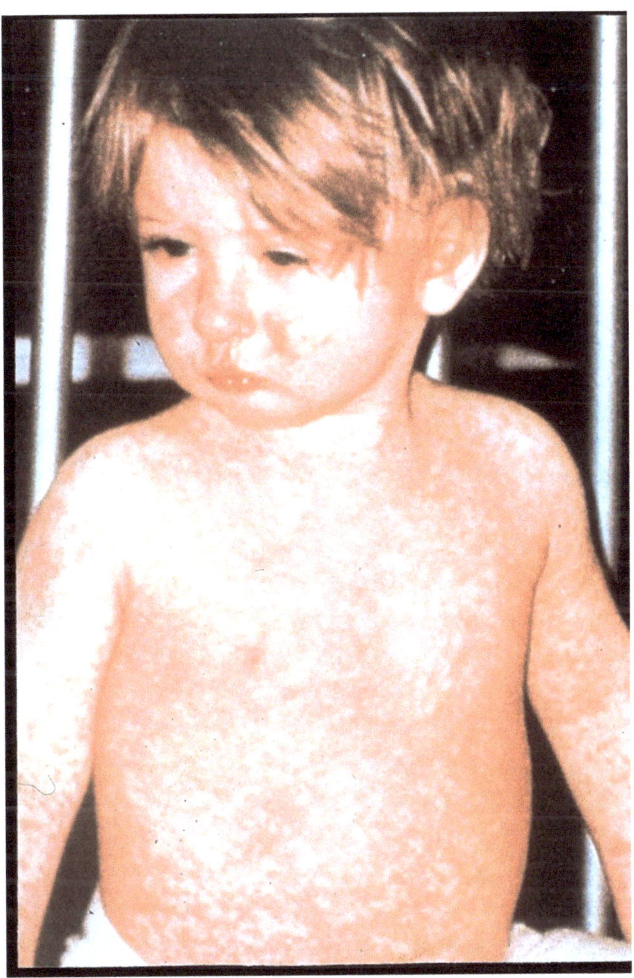

Measles rash covering child's arms and stomach (Source: Centers for Disease Control and Prevention)

- **Whooping cough** (pertussis) is a highly contagious disease that can be deadly to babies. Whooping cough causes uncontrollable, violent coughing which makes it hard to breath. The "whooping" name comes from the sharp inhalation after a coughing fit. This disease can also cause life threatening pauses in breathing with no cough at all (apnea).

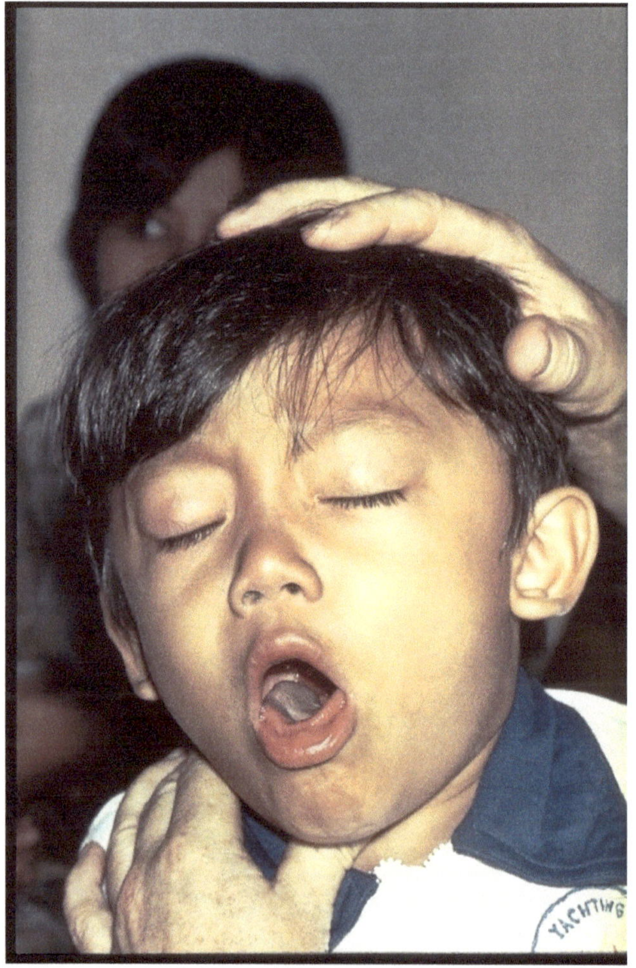

Child has pertussis; it is difficult for him to stop coughing and to get air (Source: Centers for Disease Control and Prevention)

- **Meningococcal meningitis** is a bacterial infection that causes the membranes that cover the brain and spinal cord to become inflamed. The infection can also leak into the blood (meningococcemia).

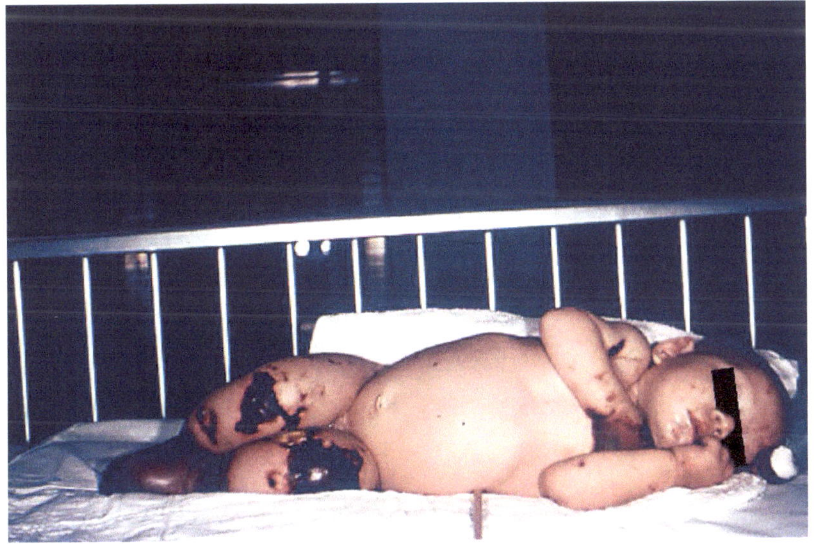

Four-month-old female with gangrene of hands and lower extremities due to meningococcemia (Source: Centers for Disease Control and Prevention)

- **Rotavirus** is contagious and causes severe watery diarrhoea, abdominal pain, vomiting and fever. The child becomes severely dehydrated and this can lead to death.

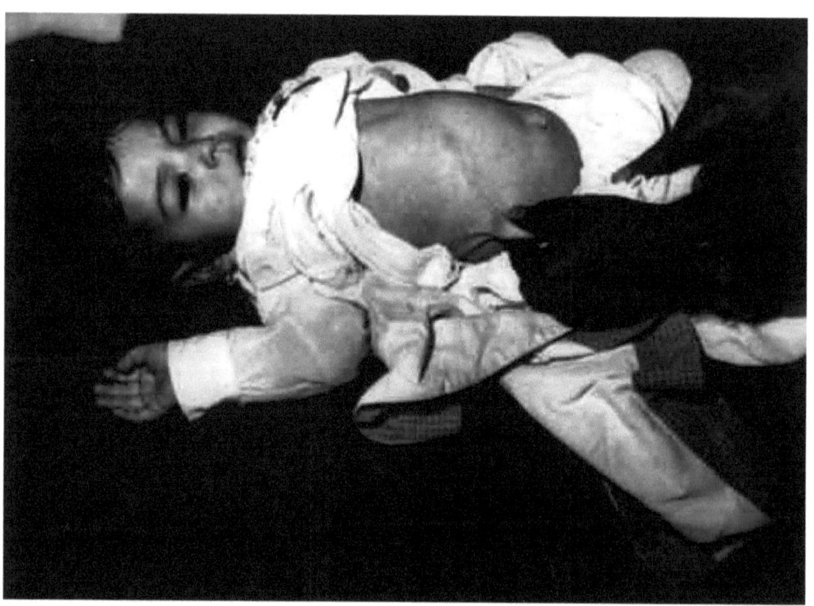

Doctor examining a dehydrated child (Source: Centers for Disease Control and Prevention)

- **Mumps** causes puffy cheeks and a swollen jaw, caused by swelling of the salivary glands. Other symptoms include headache, muscle ache, fever and tiredness. The mumps virus can also cause infertility in males.

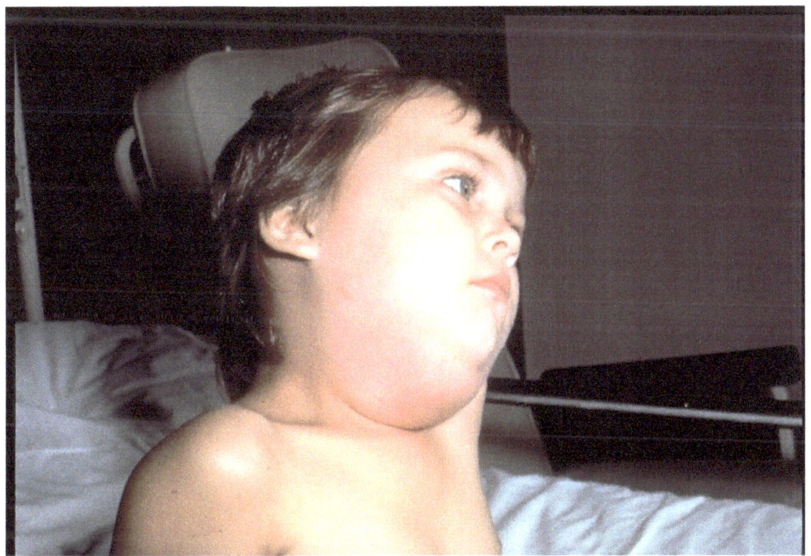

Child very swollen under the jaw and in the cheeks due to mumps (Source: Centers for Disease Control and Prevention)

- **Chicken pox** causes an itchy blistery rash all over the body and includes fever. Scratching the blisters leads to scarring.

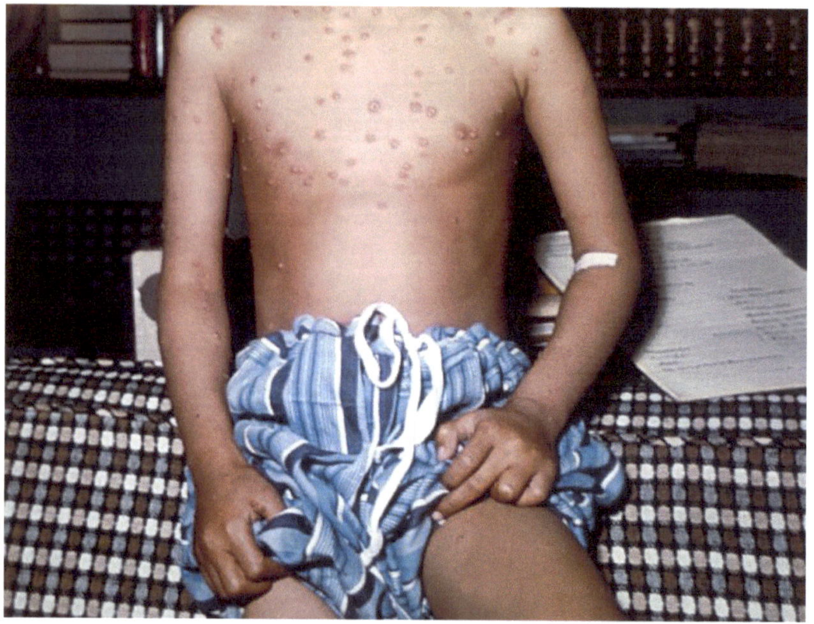

Chickenpox lesions on torso of four-year-old child, day 5 of illness (Source: Centers for Disease Control and Prevention)

- **Diphtheria** causes a thick covering at the back of the nose and throat that makes breathing and swallowing difficult. Diphtheria can also lead to heart failure, paralysis and death.

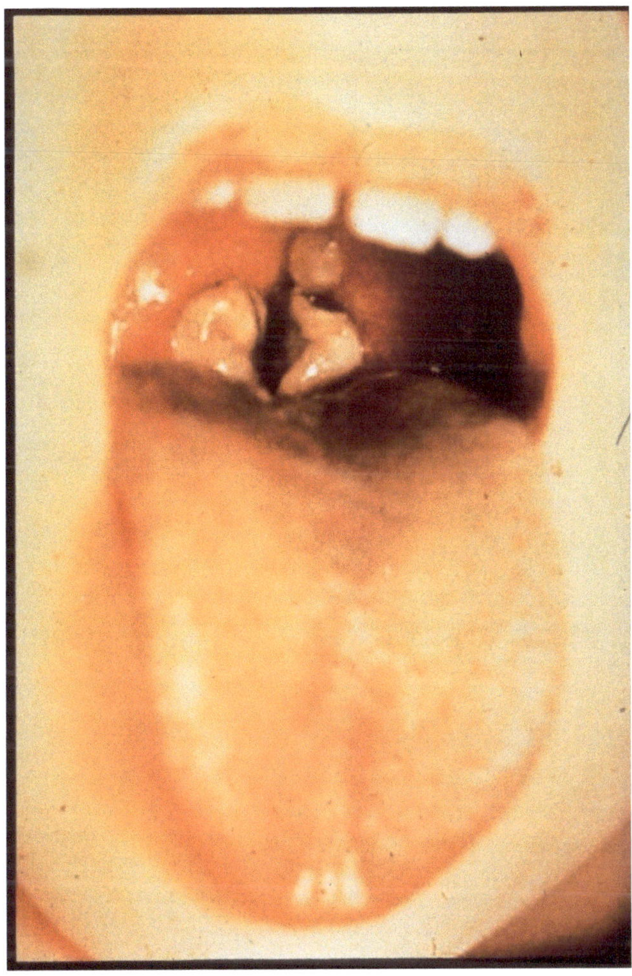

Child has diphtheria, thick gray coating over back of throat (Source: Centers for Disease Control and Prevention)

- **Smallpox** is a contagious, disfiguring and deadly disease that has affected humans for thousands of years. Smallpox was eradicated worldwide by 1980 – the result of an unprecedented global immunization campaign.

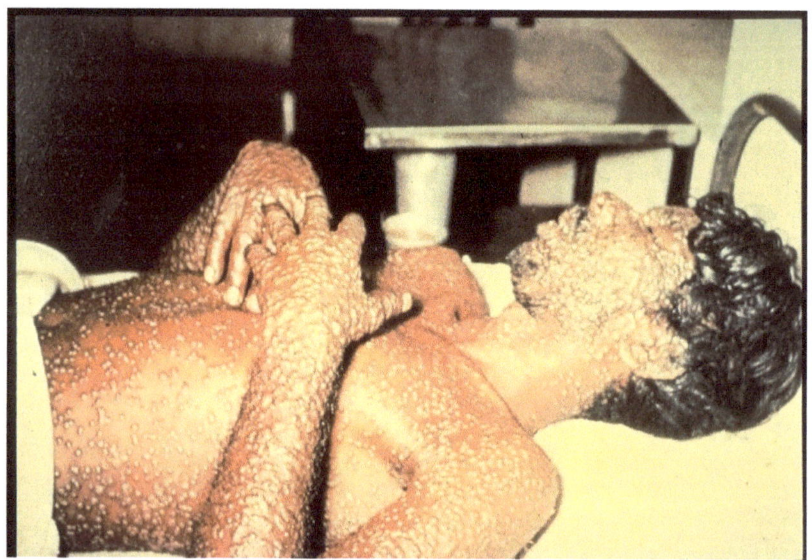

Man has smallpox; body is covered with smallpox lesions (Source: Centers for Disease Control and Prevention)

Anti-vaxxer's are in the process of destroying humanity's herd immunity. We are in danger of losing our children to horrific, deadly diseases that were once preventable. Not all vaccines can be administered at birth. This is because a baby's immunity is immature, and the immunity needs time to produce antibodies to the first vaccine before the next set is administered.

Without herd immunity, humanity will return to the pre-vaccine era, before the 18th century, when children suffered disfigurements, scars, paralysis, and died in agony.

In addition to vaccinations, society has a further responsibility to live financially well within their means, and to live in homes that are ethically constructed without harm to the environment or habitat or forests.

Society is falling in love with the **tiny house movement**. This movement encourages living a simpler life in smaller spaces. People from all walks of life are finding that large homes are costly and detrimental to the environment. A tiny house on wheels can also be beneficial during disasters, such as floods and hurricanes, because it can be towed away from danger, as can be seen below. It is also built at a fraction of the cost of a conventional house.

Tiny houses on display during Build Small Live Large 2017 in Portland, OR Attribution: DanDavidCook / CC BY-SA (https://creativecommons.org/licenses/by-sa/4.0)

One doesn't need to compromise on anything when living in a tiny house. All the amenities are incorporated either inside or outside the tiny house. Because the costs of building and taking care of a tiny house is low, one doesn't need to pursue the rat race template of finding the most well-paid job, finding the largest home and car, and then to retire at the age of 65 years, with inadequate retirement funds.

For most Americans, a third to a half of their salaries is used to provide a roof over their heads, and most will need to figure out how to afford the house and car that society dictates. Because of this rat race, the majority of Americans are living from pay check to pay check. Can you imagine spending only 15 dollars on utilities every month, in addition to the joy of living close to nature and forests, as can be seen below.

Example of a tiny home built amidst nature.
Attribution: Ben Chun / CC BY-SA
(https://creativecommons.org/licenses/by-sa/2.0)

Every tiny house looks different because it looks at living on your unique terms. Tiny house owners are unlikely to have a mortgage or credit card debt and have more saved up cash, than conventional homeowners. A tiny home is easier to maintain and quicker to clean, and see how spacious it is inside: https://www.homestratosphere.com/tiny-home-designs/.

The limitations to tiny-house-living is access to land. Land is in short supply, and tiny house owners are looking for the balance of being close to work and being away from the cities. Banks don't feel that the resale value is good on a tiny house, which means that acquiring a mortgage for a tiny house is impossible.

Many municipalities have minimum square meter requirements for a house because they like the higher tax assessment. They insist on electricity, water and sewer fees, even though the tiny house consists of a composting toilet, off grid water, and off grid electricity supply. Municipalities don't actually want tiny houses.

The only way the tiny house movement is going to succeed is if people or governments buy land with the intention of building tiny house communities. This concept can also be used to solve the problem of inadequate housing as well as the problem of slum living.

The launch of the Social Bite Homeless Tiny House Village in Edinburgh UK
May 17th 2018
Attribution: Cavajunky / CC BY-SA
(https://creativecommons.org/licenses/by-sa/4.0)

Governments no longer need to fund conventional homes for the poor, but can build off grid tiny houses, built amid farms, gardens and forests maintained by the tiny house communities. Imagine if you could provide community-focused housing for the poor… like the tiny house village called Quixote Village in Olympia, Washington (http://www.quixotecommunities.org/olympia-quixote-village.html).

The people who live in this village for the poor pay a third of their income for the upkeep of the community. The community is also substance and alcohol free. Tiny house communities create microcosms of peace, shelter and adventure within nature.

Society, this is a call to care for the herd to ensure that our young and weak are protected from diseases, by ensuring that entire populations are vaccinated. When humanity is vaccinated it creates strength in numbers and affords us an opportunity to raise all our children to adulthood.

Society, this is a call to care for our planet by living in harmony with nature amid gardens and farms in a home that is modern, fully functional, renewable and off grid.

Society, your purpose is to empower humanity! Let's take care of our herd in a dignified manner through ethics and collaboration!

TECHNOLOGY: A CALL TO INVEST

Photo by Lucien Wanda from Pexels

Plastic is everywhere! From inside the stomachs of whales, to the deep oceans, to the fish we eat, and even in our own bodies. Marine life that consumes jelly fish, perceive plastic to be jelly fish and consume plastic in large quantities.

The eight billion tons of plastic that humanity has already created is expected to triple by 2050. Some plastics are recyclable, but ninety percent is not. Plastic that is not recyclable lands up in landfills where it can take a thousand years to completely degrade. By 2050, there will be more plastic in the ocean than fish. Bans on plastic straws and fees for plastic bags are not going to stop the suffering of animals from plastic pollution.

For about every natural material on earth, like bone, there is an organism to break it down. The reason why plastic takes such a long time to degrade is that it has not been around humanity for very long, only fifty years, and plastic contains chemicals that nature has never seen before.

In 2016, **Japanese** scientists discovered a new bacterium that could digest plastic. It was discovered near a bottle recycling plant in Japan in a plastic dumpsite. The bacterium is called Ideonella sakaiensis and it digests polyethylene terephthalate (PET). PET is the most common plastic in the world and is used to make soda bottles, blister packs, food containers, and even shirts and dresses.

In the **UK**, while studying the plastic digesting enzyme from Ideonella sakaiensis, the scientists modified the enzyme to determine how it evolved and accidentally created a better enzyme, one that digested plastic in days rather than weeks. In the US, scientists are working on making this enzyme, called PETase, work faster.

Using PETase in the environment is complicated because the team will have to demonstrate that the degradation of plastic does not come at the cost of bringing about an unforeseen negative effect on the environment. Scientists say that bringing such a plastic bio-digester into the market is still years away because more funding is required.

Other scientists are handling the problem differently. The scientists at **Purdue University**, USA, are turning the plastic in foam into fuel. The French company **Carbios** has already demonstrated that they can break PET into its smaller, original components. This can then be recycled to make new plastic removing the need to use fossil fuel to make plastic. This recycling bioreactor will also take years to come online, because more funding is required.

Digesting plastic is only a small part of removing plastic from the environment. Scientists can't just release solutions like PETase into the oceans or the rivers or in the wild, it may not work outside of a test environment, and it may have unintended consequences. It's far more controllable to treat plastic in landfills.

A **South African** company is helping to deal with the country's waste problem by taking plastic milk bottles from landfills and using them to build roads. In 2019 this South African company, Shisalanga, has become the first in Africa to lay a section of road that is part plastic. It has already repaved four hundred meters of road using asphalt, made with forty thousand recycled two Litre plastic milk bottles.

A recycling plant in South Africa turns the plastic milk bottles into pellets, which are treated to a hundred and ninety degrees Celsius, until they dissolve. The plastic component is then used to replace the asphalt's bitumen binder. **Shisalanga** says that this plastic component produces fewer toxic emissions than the traditional component, and that this road surface is much more durable and water resistant and is expected to last longer.

Shisalanga, is currently researching the use of non-recyclable plastic from landfills allowing the company to remove even more from landfills for repurposing.

Plastic in the ocean is being removed by scientists from the Netherlands. An enormous floating device designed by **Dutch** scientists for the non-profit organization Ocean Cleanup successfully captured and removed plastic from the Pacific Ocean for the first time in 2019. The 'giant arm' net-device captures large cartons, crates, abandoned fishing gear, as well as micro-plastics. Once the plastic is collected it is returned to land and processed for recycling.

Another important technological advancement that needs investment is **carbon dioxide removal technologies**. Even if we cut our carbon dioxide emissions to zero, emissions from agriculture and air travel will still produce carbon dioxide. Carbon dioxide that is already in the atmosphere can affect the climate for thousands of years. Carbon dioxide removal technologies will, therefore, be critical to remove a thousand gigatons of carbon dioxide this century.

Carbon mineralization makes use of a natural process of reacting peridodite, or basaltic lava, with carbon dioxide to form solid carbonate minerals, such as limestone, and this limestone can store carbon dioxide for millions of years. The reactive materials are combined with carbon dioxide containing fluid at carbon capture stations, or the fluid can be pumped into reactive rock formations where they naturally occur.

Scientists in the US are finding ways to speed up the natural reaction to increase carbon dioxide uptake, as well as looking at the feasibility of storing fifty million tons of carbon dioxide in basalt reservoirs of the Pacific Northwest. Beneath two thousand six hundred meters of water, and another two hundred meters of sediment, the basalt reservoir contains spaces that will fill up as the carbon dioxide mineralises into carbonated limestone. The next step is to pilot this project, which is key for technical as well as regulatory reasons and this project requires funding for the pilot project to begin.

Direct air capture sucks carbon dioxide out of the air by using fans to move air over substances that bind to carbon dioxide. The technology makes use of compounds in a liquid solution, or in a coating, that captures carbon dioxide as they come into contact with it and it is then treated and stored underground.

The benefits of direct air capture are that it removes carbon dioxide that is already in the atmosphere, and the system can be installed anywhere. At a coal plant, one in ten molecules of emitted gas is carbon dioxide. In the atmosphere, one in two thousand five hundred molecules is carbon dioxide, which means that carbon dioxide is less concentrated in the atmosphere than in the exhaust fumes from a coal plant. It is therefore more difficult to remove carbon dioxide from the atmosphere than from an exhaust pipe.

Climeworks (Switzerland) captures a thousand metric tons of carbon dioxide a year. Climeworks now has fourteen direct to air plants built or under construction in Europe. A plant in Italy makes methane fuel for trucks from captured carbon dioxide.

Carbon Engineering (Canada) captures one million tons of carbon dioxide a year. This company's strategy is to turn the captured carbon dioxide into carbon neutral synthetic hydrocarbon fuels. **Global Thermostat** (USA) aims to sell the captured carbon dioxide to a soda factory, with the intention that each soda factory will eventually have their own direct air capture plants.

The projection is that the direct air capture process will suck up 5 gigatons of carbon dioxide a year by 2050, but this process is still in the early stages of development and requires funding.

Governments, corporates and environmental charities, this is a call to invest in new technology, to invest in pilot projects, to take new technological developments to the consumer, and to **educate** them on environmentally better options so that they can support the product.

Governments, producers, researchers and recyclers, this is a call to invest in recycling non-recyclable plastics, and to process plastic landfills by 2025, so that the land can be better used for environmentally friendly projects.

Governments, businesses, researchers and manufacturers, this is a call to invest in carbon dioxide reversal projects because our planet already has high carbon dioxide levels.

Governments, producers, recyclers, business and manufacturers: your purpose is to operate in a disciplined and ethical way to give the consumers what they need and not what they want, by prioritising the environment over profit!

LAW: A CALL FOR SANCTIONS

Norway, Iceland, and Japan are the only three countries that hunt **whales** commercially. While the 1986 International Whaling Commission (IWC) banned commercial whaling, this is not being enforced. Norway continues to ignore the moratorium and, in 2018, increased the quota to hunt 1278 whales. In fact, Norway has surpassed Japan and Iceland, and is the country that kills the most whales in the world.

Whales are migratory. They migrate to feed, and they migrate to breed. Killing whales in Japan, Iceland, and Norway, will therefore reduce the global population. Iceland temporarily stopped whaling in the summer of 2019, due to a lack of demand for whale meat, while Japan has cut back on whaling to focus on whaling in its own waters. Whaling does still happen in neighbouring waters, however, under the guise of "research".

An adult and sub-adult Minke whale are dragged aboard the Nisshin Maru, a Japanese whaling vessel. The wound that is visible on the calf's side was reportedly caused by an explosive-packed harpoon.
Attribution: Australian Customs and Border Protection Service / CC BY-SA 3.0 AU (https://creativecommons.org/licenses/by-sa/3.0/au/deed.en)

Norway has continued a business-as-usual attitude, increasing the number of whales hunted year on year, receiving little pressure from the IWC or from other countries. Interestingly, the demand for whale meat in Norway is low, so Norway researches new ways to use the carcass. A lot of the whale meat is exported to Japan, sent to tourist restaurants and to cruise ships.

Norway fishermen are of the belief that whales eat all the fish in the ocean and that by removing them from the food chain, there will be plenty more fish in the ocean. The reason why fish stocks are low is because of humans overfishing them. Very few know that whale faeces play an important role in providing nourishment for plankton and without whales, plankton will die out.

Norway also obscures the inhumane methods of hunting these mammals. Grenades are harpooned into the whale which explodes twelve inches into the body of the whale releasing sharp claws that tear the flesh of the animal. This method of hunting leads to a slow, deeply painful death for the whale.

What is even more grisly, is that the Norwegian hunter prefers to hunt the pregnant females because these are easier to catch and the pregnant females offer two whales for the price of one.

Another apex predator that needs full protection from hunters are sharks. **Sharks** are not hunted for their meat, but for their fins. Shark finning is cruel, because the fisherman hunts the shark, hacks off its fins while it is alive and then disposes of the live, dying shark back into the ocean.

Sharks are important for the ocean because they keep marine species in-check and thereby keeps the ocean clean. For example, in areas where shark numbers have declined, mid-level predators, like snappers, increased, which in turn shrank the herbivorous fish stock that the snappers fed on. With fewer algae-eating fish around, the algae overwhelmed the reefs and the waters. Sharks also feed on dead matter on the ocean floor, keeping the ocean floor clean.

Sharks also hold cures for diseases. It has puzzled researchers for years why sharks don't get sick. Shark tissue has anticoagulant and antibacterial properties. Scientists are studying sharks in the hope of finding new treatments for viruses and even pulmonary fibrosis.

The drug, **AD-114**, has been developed by researchers at Melbourne University in collaboration with the biotechnology company AdAlta. The drug has been inspired by the antibodies in shark blood and can destroy the cells that cause fibrosis. No sharks were harmed in this process as it only required that a single blood sample be taken from the Wobbegong shark. This sample has led to the creation of a human protein that imitates the shark antibody.

Shark skin's unique antimicrobial properties have also led to the creation of an antibacterial product called **Sharklet AF**. This product is used on in-hospital patients to ward off superbugs.

Sharks add more value alive, than dead and therefore shark finning must be banned. Humans kill a hundred million sharks a year, primarily in **China** and **Vietnam**. Sharks don't have the biology to sustain high levels of fishing, because they grow slowly, have relatively few young, and take a long time to mature. If they are overfished, their species collapses.

The King Diamond II was seized in 2002 while carrying over 32 short tons (29 metric tons) of shark fins that were harvested from about 30,000 sharks.
Attribution: Unknown members of U.S. Coast Guard / Public domain

Interestingly, shark tourism boosts economies. Shark tourism generates more than three hundred million US dollars annually and this figure is predicted to double in the next twenty years. This industry provides ten thousand jobs in twenty-nine countries. A hundred million sharks are killed per year – and yet they are worth more alive than dead.

In addition to applying sanctions to China and Vietnam, many educational campaigns are required to highlight the dangers of eating shark fins. Shark fins contains high levels of mercury and, therefore, makes it an unhealthy meat to eat. Mercury is neurotoxic and causes infertility. It can also damage the lungs and the kidneys, as well as damaging hearing and vision. What is worse is that mothers with mercury poisoning give birth to babies with birth defects.

How does mercury get into the oceans in the first place? Burning coal releases a hundred and sixty tons of mercury into the air, per year, in the USA alone. Rainfall washes the mercury into the ocean. Once in the ocean, mercury is converted to monomethyl mercury

(MMHg) and this form of mercury is toxic. MMHg then diffuses into plankton and passes up the food chain, with concentrations of MMHg increasing up the food chain.

MMHg concentrations in carnivorous fish such as freshwater bass, pike, shark and swordfish are up to a million times greater in the fish than in the surrounding water.

It is hard to believe how low the mercury concentration needs to be to cause great illness. Consumption of a two hundred and forty millilitre volume of shark fin soup contains on average 4.6 ng/mL of toxic monomethylmercury (MMHg). Blood levels in the 30 to 40 ng/mL range causes the person to become symptomatic with brain and kidney damage. Blood levels above 100 ng/mL is considered mercury poisoning.

Countries, this is a call to impose sanctions on countries that kill sharks and whales. Some species are critically endangered, and the species still have to overcome climate change. Imposing sanctions is an essential act because these animals provide essential services to the ocean.

Norway, Iceland, China, Vietnam and Japan (and other countries) this is a call to stop your killing spree. Whales and sharks are worth more alive than dead. Preserve these magnificent animals for our oceans, where they belong. Train the fishermen on the value that these species add to the planet, then give the fishermen work in your newly created shark and whale tourism industry.

Countries, your purpose is to focus on ethics by increasing shark and whale numbers even though you have come to depend on killing sharks and whales for your livelihood! Network with other countries, like South Africa and Canada, to learn how they have turned sharks and whales into tourism.

ENVIRONMENT: A CALL TO PROTECT

Thirty percent of the world's crops and ninety percent of all plants require cross pollination to spread and thrive. **Bees** are our most important pollinators and, unfortunately, bee populations are declining around the world.

Climate change causes some flowers to bloom later or earlier than usual, leaving bees with fewer food sources. Bees suffer habitat loss from human developments or the lack of bee friendly flowers. Some colonies collapse due to plants and seeds treated with **neonicotinoid** pesticides. These pesticides harm bees by impairing their learning and memory, and these are key features that play a role in colony fitness as they facilitate foraging.

Apples, melons, asparagus, berries, broccoli, almonds, peaches, and watermelon, for example, require bees for cross pollination. As bees forage for nectar to produce honey, they cross pollinate pollen from the anther of one flower to the stigma of another flower. In so doing, the flower is fertilised, and the fruit or vegetable is produced.

It's not only farmed crops that need bees for pollination; many species of wild plants depend on insect pollinators as well. These plants will, after having been pollinated, produce wild seeds and fruit that feed wild animals.

Honeybee with pollen baskets
Attribution: Ivar Leidus / CC BY-SA
(https://creativecommons.org/licenses/by-sa/4.0)

Bees also produce honey to feed their colonies during the cold months. Honey is also a food source for many other animals. A bee, itself, is part of the food chain as insects and birds feed on bees.

Their role as pollinators is vital in the growth of tropical forests, woodlands, and deciduous forests. Many tree species couldn't grow without bees. If bees disappeared, not only will the crop and plants and trees disappear, but the animals that depend on those plants and trees will also disappear.

With global warming and climate change, pests are becoming prolific. This means that the farmer will use more pesticide and more bee colonies will collapse. Data shows that even wildflowers are infected with pesticides, even though it is not targeted by farmers.

In **Slovenia,** the bee population is on the increase where beekeeping has always been a way of life. In this small European country of two million people, one in every two hundred people is a beekeeper. During the Covid lockdown, the government deemed beekeepers as essential workers, permitting them to travel freely to tend to their hives. Bees are themselves essential workers in making life possible for humans.

From 2007 to 2017, Slovenia saw a 57% increase in beehive numbers. Slovenian beekeepers are not supportive of bees for the sale of honey for money, they take care of bees because they love them. When the Beekeepers Association noticed a decline in bee numbers, they suspected the neonicotinoid pesticides were the cause and urged the Ministry of Agriculture to ban them. A farmer found to be using banned pesticides became subject to fines. Immediately after the ban, beekeepers reported fewer bee deaths.

The Slovenian approach to beekeeping is to conserve, protect and breed the indigenous Slovenian honeybee and to ban the import of other honeybee species that bring in new diseases. Importing honeybees has been found to be problematic to beekeepers because they struggle to adapt to their new environment and then become vulnerable to disease. With climate change, foreign bees are less able to adapt.

In Slovenia, the beekeeper makes use of the "AZ" hives, which looks more like cabinets, allowing the beekeeper to monitor these smaller hives more closely. They also protect hives from harsh winters and strong wind. Colonies kept in denser, industrialised settings than they would be found in nature and are moved around on a single plot of land develop more parasites and diseases.

"File:Beehives in Slovenia (4913661031).jpg" by david_jones is licensed under CC BY 2.0

In the US, beekeepers keep thousands of hives. In Slovenia, beekeepers don't keep more than a hundred hives so that they can monitor and take complete care of their bees. This method of beekeeping is more time consuming, but essential during climate change and when bee numbers are declining.

The Slovenian government created the Beekeeping Academy of Slovenia in April 2018, to educate beekeepers from around the world, and are fostering international interest in bee conservation. The UN approved Slovenia's proposal to proclaim the 20th of May as World Bee Day. The purpose of this international day is to acknowledge and preserve the role of bees in the ecosystem.

Countries, this is a call to preserve and grow indigenous bee communities and to ban neonicotinoid pesticides immediately.

Bee farmers, this is a call to stop importing non-native bees because they struggle to survive in new environments, are not resistant to climate change, and bring foreign diseases to the local bees.

Bee farmers, this is a call to manage no more than a hundred bee colonies, per farm and to use only the Slovenian "AZ" cabinet hives.

Government and farmers, your purpose is to ban neonicotinoid pesticides immediately and to learn from and use Slovenia's proven bee-keeping methods!

EPILOGUE

Our planet is a terribly sick patient! She needs oxygen, and is gasping for breath, because she has inhaled noxious fumes. She has a high fever and her natural self defence mechanisms have been eroded. She has numerous viral and tick infections and refuses to be vaccinated.

She continues to deplete her dwindling food supply, and stupidly spills all her drinking water onto the floor, even though she is severely dehydrated. She destroyed her plant- and animal-sourced medicine, and her bodily fluids are seeping into her bed linen. She also cancelled her entertainment subscription and even thought that swallowing plastic will be okay...and now she is choking on it.

These are the 10 steps necessary to keep her alive...

Step 1: Let's open her airway by removing all plastic from the ocean and by recycling and processing all landfills as quickly as we can. Let's also only manufacture biodegradable plastics from now on.

Step 2: Let's remove the noxious fumes and administer oxygen by planting Miyawaki forests urgently to absorb carbon dioxide and to supply oxygen. Let's stop the production of the noxious gases by implementing renewable energy sources of electricity.

Step 3: Let's hydrate her by removing high-water requiring crops and replacing these with crops that are nutritious and drought tolerant.

Step 4: Let's treat our patient medicinally by preserving the fauna and flora (and their pollinators) in the oceans and in the forests.

Step 5: Let's give her nourishment by being Smart about growing food and by banning neonicotinoid pesticides, immediately.

Step 6: Let's vaccinate her to prevent her from succumbing to viruses and ticks and to make her resilient to further infections.

Step 7: Let's renew her food sources by not fishing from the oceans any longer and by using renewable aquaculture techniques.

Step 8: Let's clean up her bed linen by building tiny houses that are off grid to preserve her integrity and to improve her peace of mind.

Step 9: Let's entertain her by taking her to Norway and China to watch the whale and shark numbers rise in their natural habitat.

Step 10: And as she responds to these treatments, her fever will subside…

REFERENCES:

https://www.theguardian.com/environment/2020/may/07/promiscuous-treatment-of-nature-will-lead-to-more-pandemics-scientists

https://www.motherjones.com/environment/2020/05/these-scientists-saw-covid-19-coming-now-theyre-trying-to-stop-the-next-pandemic-before-it-starts/

https://www.euronews.com/2020/05/22/euronews-holds-live-debate-on-climate-change-and-its-threat-to-our-health

https://edition.cnn.com/2020/05/08/weather/killer-heat-climate-change-study/index.html

https://www.clickenergy.com.au/news-blog/12-countries-leading-the-way-in-renewable-energy

https://energynews.us/2013/10/17/midwest/is-burning-garbage-green-in-sweden-theres-little-debate/

https://www.vox.com/science-and-health/2019/11/18/20970604/amazon-rainforest-2019-brazil-burning-deforestation-bolsonaro

https://www.wbur.org/cognoscenti/2019/06/05/climate-change-food-frederick-hewett

https://www.naturespath.com/en-us/blog/climate-change-is-here-and-its-becoming-harder-to-farm-successfully/

https://wwf.panda.org/knowledge_hub/where_we_work/amazon/amazon_threats/climate_change_amazon/

https://tree-nation.com/projects

https://daily.jstor.org/the-miyawaki-method-a-better-way-to-build-forests/

https://e360.yale.edu/features/soil_as_carbon_storehouse_new_weapon_in_climate_fight

https://bengaluru.citizenmatters.in/how-to-make-mini-forest-miyawaki-method-34867

https://smartfarming.co.za

http://www.fao.org/3/ca3718en/ca3718en.pdf

https://www.auroras.eu/internet-of-things-in-agriculture-how-countries-support-smart-farming/

https://claroenergy.in/5-most-water-intensive-crops/

https://gilmour.com/drought-tolerant-vegetable-garden

https://www.thebalance.com/top-aquaculture-countries-1301739

https://www.quora.com/What-countries-are-the-most-guilty-of-overfishing-today

https://globallymealliance.org/news/global-warming-means-pathogens/

https://www.livescience.com/32617-how-do-vaccines-work.html

https://en.wikipedia.org/wiki/Herd_immunity

https://www.cdc.gov/vaccines/parents/diseases/forgot-14-diseases.html

https://www.darkdaily.com/australias-hpv-vaccination-program-could-eliminate-cervical-cancer-if-its-national-hpv-vaccination-and-screening-programs-remain-on-current-pace/

https://thetinylife.com/what-is-the-tiny-house-movement/

https://en.wikipedia.org/wiki/Tiny_house_movement

https://www.vox.com/the-highlight/2019/4/9/18274131/plastic-waste-pollution-bacteria-digestion

https://blogs.ei.columbia.edu/2018/11/27/carbon-dioxide-removal-climate-change/

https://endplasticwaste.org/about-the-alliance-to-end-plastic-waste/

https://edition.cnn.com/2019/10/30/business/plastic-roads-in-south-africa-intl/index.html

https://www.wildaboutwhales.com.au/whale-facts/about-whales/whale-migration

https://uk.whales.org/our-4-goals/stop-whaling/whaling-in-norway/

http://savedolphins.eii.org/news/entry/norway-now-kills-more-whales-than-japan

https://www.livescience.com/8788-whale-poo-ocean-miracle-grow.html

https://www.conservation.org/blog/5-things-you-didnt-know-sharks-do-for-you

http://thewanderingwalker.com/many-important-reasons-ban-shark-finning/

https://www.greenprophet.com/2012/01/shark-fin-mercury-poisoning/

https://www.marchofdimes.org/pregnancy/mercury.aspx#

https://www.nationwidechildrens.org/family-resources-education/700childrens/2016/07/the-dangers-of-mercury-and-how-to-get-rid-of-it-safely

https://www.urmc.rochester.edu/encyclopedia/content.aspx?contenttypeid=167&contentid=mercury_blood

https://dec.vermont.gov/waste-management/solid/product-stewardship/mercury/fish

https://www.whoi.edu/oceanus/feature/how-does-toxic-mercury-get-into-fish/

https://wildaid.org/wp-content/uploads/2018/02/WildAid-Sharks-in-Crisis-2018.pdf

https://www.pthomeandgarden.com/5-ways-bees-are-important-to-the-environment/

https://jeb.biologists.org/content/218/20/3199

https://bees.techno-science.ca/english/bees/pollination/food-depends-on-bees.php

https://qz.com/107970/scientists-discover-whats-killing-the-bees-and-its-worse-than-you-thought/

https://insh.world/science/what-if-we-lost-the-amazon-rainforest/

https://www.bbc.com/news/world-australia-38792405

https://time.com/5815141/slovenia-bees-climate-change/